This book belongs to:

_____

_____

_____

Friends

An address book for those who
cherish the joys of friendship

Illustrated by
Donna Green

VERMILION

This edition published in 1996 by Vermilion, Inc.
P.O. Box 176, Cohasset, MA 02025

If you would like to own a limited-edition signed and numbered reproduction
of a painting by artist/illustrator Donna Green, write to:
Donna Green, c/o Vermilion, Box 176, Cohasset, MA 02025

A Rob Fremont Book

Design by Berge Zerdelian
Editor: Oliver Fremont
Composition: Garbo Typesetting

ISBN: 1-883746-10-8

Printed and bound in Singapore by Imago Publishing

10 9 8 7 6 5 4 3 2 1

List of Paintings

*W*hoever is happy will make others happy too.

– ANNE FRANK

A

Name _____   Telephone _____

Address _____

_____   _____

_____   _____

_____   _____

Name _____   Telephone _____

Address _____

_____   _____

_____   _____

_____   _____

Name _____   Telephone _____

Address _____

_____   _____

_____   _____

_____   _____

Name _____   Telephone _____

Address _____

_____   _____

_____   _____

_____   _____

Name _____   Telephone _____

Address _____   _____

_____   _____

_____   _____

_____   _____

Name _____   Telephone _____

Address _____   _____

_____   _____

_____   _____

_____   _____

Name _____   Telephone _____

Address _____   _____

_____   _____

_____   _____

_____   _____

Name _____   Telephone _____

Address _____   _____

_____   _____

_____   _____

_____   _____

Friendship with oneself is all important, because without it one cannot be friends with anyone else in the world. – ELEANOR ROOSEVELT

Name

Telephone

Address

Name

Telephone

Address

Name

Telephone

Address

Name

Telephone

Address

A

Name _____ Telephone _____

Address _____ _____

_____ _____

_____ _____

Name _____ Telephone _____

Address _____ _____

_____ _____

_____ _____

Name _____ Telephone _____

Address _____ _____

_____ _____

_____ _____

Name _____ Telephone _____

Address _____ _____

_____ _____

_____ _____

Name _____ Telephone _____

Address _____ _____

_____ _____

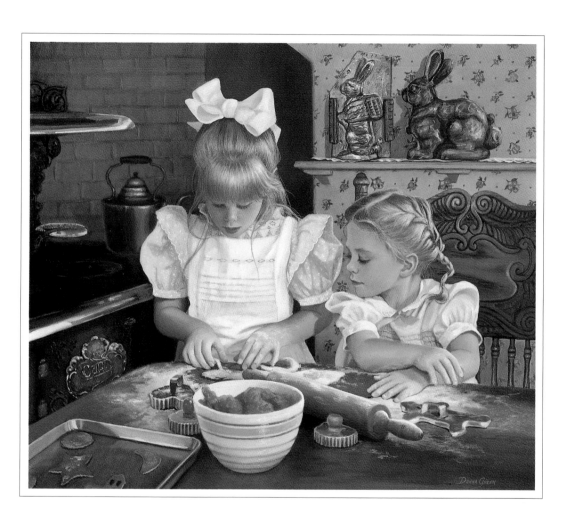

A friend is a present you give yourself.
– ROBERT LOUIS STEVENSON

A

Name _____ Telephone _____

Address _____ _____

_____ _____

_____ _____

Name _____ Telephone _____

Address _____ _____

_____ _____

_____ _____

Name _____ Telephone _____

Address _____ _____

_____ _____

_____ _____

Name _____ Telephone _____

Address _____ _____

_____ _____

_____ _____

Name _____ Telephone _____

Address _____ _____

_____ _____

_____ _____

Name _____ Telephone _____

Address _____ _____

_____ _____

_____ _____

Name _____ Telephone _____

Address _____ _____

_____ _____

_____ _____

Name _____ Telephone _____

Address _____ _____

_____ _____

_____ _____

Name _____ Telephone _____

Address _____ _____

_____ _____

_____ _____

"Stay" is a charming word in a friend's vocabulary.
–LOUISA MAY ALCOTT

B

Name _____   Telephone _____

Address _____   _____

_____   _____

_____   _____

_____   _____

Name _____   Telephone _____

Address _____   _____

_____   _____

_____   _____

_____   _____

Name _____   Telephone _____

Address _____   _____

_____   _____

_____   _____

_____   _____

Name _____   Telephone _____

Address _____   _____

_____   _____

_____   _____

Name _____ Telephone _____

Address _____ _____

_____ _____

_____ _____

Name _____ Telephone _____

Address _____ _____

_____ _____

_____ _____

Name _____ Telephone _____

Address _____ _____

_____ _____

_____ _____

Name _____ Telephone _____

Address _____ _____

_____ _____

_____ _____

As *you say, we don't need soft skies to make friendship a joy to us. What a heavenly thing it is; "World without end," truly. I grow warm thinking of it, and should glow at the thought if all the glaciers of the Alps were heaped over me!* —CELIA THAXTER

Name _____   *Telephone* _____

Address _____   _____

_____   _____

_____   _____

Name _____   *Telephone* _____

Address _____   _____

_____   _____

_____   _____

Name _____   *Telephone* _____

Address _____   _____

_____   _____

_____   _____

Name _____   *Telephone* _____

Address _____   _____

_____   _____

_____   _____

Name _____   *Telephone* _____

Address _____   _____

_____   _____

_____   _____

Name _____   *Telephone* _____

Address _____   _____

_____   _____

_____   _____

Name _____   *Telephone* _____

Address _____   _____

_____   _____

_____   _____

Name _____   *Telephone* _____

Address _____   _____

_____   _____

_____   _____

Make happy those who are near, and those who are far will come.
– CHINESE PROVERB

B

Name _____

Telephone _____

Address _____

_____

_____

_____

_____

_____

Name _____

Telephone _____

Address _____

_____

_____

_____

_____

_____

Name _____

Telephone _____

Address _____

_____

_____

_____

Name _____

Telephone _____

Address _____

_____

_____

_____

Name _____

Telephone _____

Address _____

_____

_____

*O*nce the children were in the house the air became more vivid and
more heated; every object in the house grew more alive.

– MARY GORDON

B

Name _____   Telephone _____

Address _____   _____

_____   _____

_____   _____

_____   _____

Name _____   Telephone _____

Address _____   _____

_____   _____

_____   _____

_____   _____

Name _____   Telephone _____

Address _____   _____

_____   _____

_____   _____

_____   _____

Name _____   Telephone _____

Address _____   _____

_____   _____

_____   _____

_____   _____

If we would build on a sure foundation in friendship, we must love our friends for their sakes rather than for our own.

– CHARLOTTE BRONTË

B

Name _____ Telephone _____

Address _____ _____

_____ _____

_____ _____

Name _____ Telephone _____

Address _____ _____

_____ _____

_____ _____

Name _____ Telephone _____

Address _____ _____

_____ _____

_____ _____

Name _____ Telephone _____

Address _____ _____

_____ _____

_____ _____

Name _____ Telephone _____

Address _____ _____

_____ _____

_____ _____

C

C

Name	Telephone
Address	

Name	Telephone
Address	

Name	Telephone
Address	

Name	Telephone
Address	

Name _____ *Telephone* _____

Address _____ _____

_____ _____

_____ _____

Name _____ *Telephone* _____

Address _____ _____

_____ _____

_____ _____

Name _____ *Telephone* _____

Address _____ _____

_____ _____

_____ _____

Name _____ *Telephone* _____

Address _____ _____

_____ _____

_____ _____

H*appiness is not a state to arrive at, but a manner of traveling.*
– MARGARET LEE RUNBECK

C

Name _____   Telephone _____

Address _____   _____

_____   _____

_____   _____

Name _____   Telephone _____

Address _____   _____

_____   _____

_____   _____

Name _____   Telephone _____

Address _____   _____

_____   _____

_____   _____

Name _____   Telephone _____

Address _____   _____

_____   _____

_____   _____

Name _____   Telephone _____

Address _____   _____

_____   _____

_____   _____

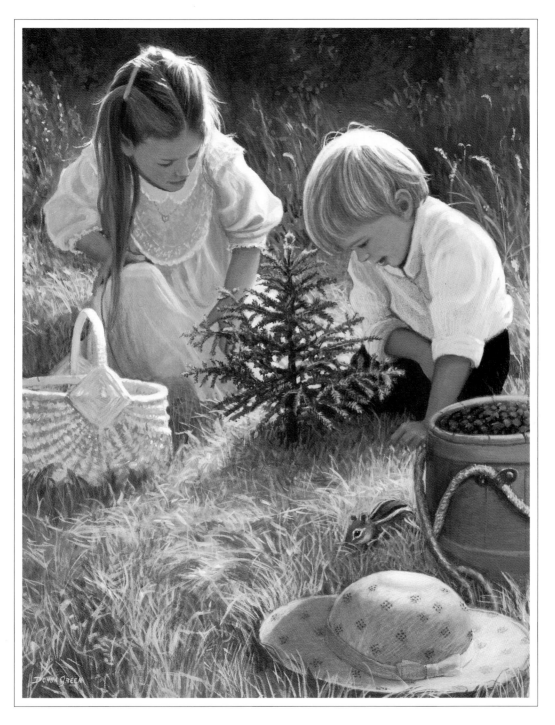

*O*n the road between the homes of friends, grass does not grow.

– NORWEGIAN PROVERB

C

Name	Telephone
Address	

Name	Telephone
Address	

Name	Telephone
Address	

Name	Telephone
Address	

Name	Telephone
Address	

Name _____   Telephone _____

Address _____   _____

_____   _____

_____   _____

_____   _____

Name _____   Telephone _____

Address _____   _____

_____   _____

_____   _____

_____   _____

Name _____   Telephone _____

Address _____   _____

_____   _____

_____   _____

_____   _____

Name _____   Telephone _____

Address _____   _____

_____   _____

_____   _____

_____   _____

You can lay the foundation of friendship in a matter of moments,
but it is a work of time to build a monument.

– MADELYN WATT

C

Name	Telephone
Address	

Name	Telephone
Address	

Name	Telephone
Address	

Name	Telephone
Address	

Name	Telephone
Address	

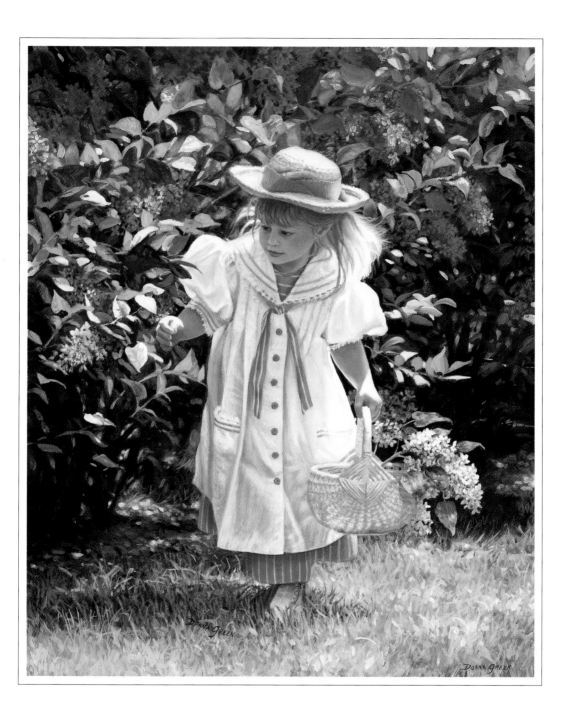

The only rose without thorns is friendship.

– MADELEINE de SCUDERY

D

D

Name _____   Telephone _____

Address _____   _____

_____   _____

_____   _____

_____   _____

Name _____   Telephone _____

Address _____   _____

_____   _____

_____   _____

_____   _____

Name _____   Telephone _____

Address _____   _____

_____   _____

_____   _____

_____   _____

Name _____   Telephone _____

Address _____   _____

_____   _____

_____   _____

Name _____ Telephone _____

Address _____ _____

_____ _____

_____ _____

Name _____ Telephone _____

Address _____ _____

_____ _____

_____ _____

Name _____ Telephone _____

Address _____ _____

_____ _____

_____ _____

Name _____ Telephone _____

Address _____ _____

_____ _____

_____ _____

N*ow may the warming love of friends*
Surround you as you go
Down the path of light and laughter
Where the happy memories grow.
–HELEN LOWRIE MARSHALL

D

Name _____   *Telephone* _____

Address _____   _____

_____   _____

_____   _____

Name _____   *Telephone* _____

Address _____   _____

_____   _____

_____   _____

Name _____   *Telephone* _____

Address _____   _____

_____   _____

_____   _____

Name _____   *Telephone* _____

Address _____   _____

_____   _____

_____   _____

Name _____ Telephone _____

Address _____ _____

_____ _____

_____ _____

Name _____ Telephone _____

Address _____ _____

_____ _____

_____ _____

Name _____ Telephone _____

Address _____ _____

_____ _____

_____ _____

Name _____ Telephone _____

Address _____ _____

_____ _____

_____ _____

W*ear a smile and have friends; Wear a scowl and have wrinkles. What do we live for if not to make the world less difficult for each other?*

– GEORGE ELIOT

D

Name	*Telephone*
Address	

Name	*Telephone*
Address	

Name	*Telephone*
Address	

Name	*Telephone*
Address	

Name	*Telephone*
Address	

*M*ake-believe colors the past with innocent distortion, and it swirls ahead of us in a thousand ways . . . It is part of our collective lives, entwining our past and our future.

– SHIRLEY TEMPLE BLACK

D

Name _____   Telephone _____

Address _____   _____

_____   _____

_____   _____

Name _____   Telephone _____

Address _____   _____

_____   _____

_____   _____

Name _____   Telephone _____

Address _____   _____

_____   _____

_____   _____

Name _____   Telephone _____

Address _____   _____

_____   _____

_____   _____

Name _____   Telephone _____

Address _____   _____

_____   _____

_____   _____

Name _____   *Telephone* _____

Address _____   _____

_____   _____

_____   _____

Name _____   *Telephone* _____

Address _____   _____

_____   _____

_____   _____

Name _____   *Telephone* _____

Address _____   _____

_____   _____

_____   _____

Name _____   *Telephone* _____

Address _____   _____

_____   _____

_____   _____

I *always felt that the great high privilege, relief and comfort of friendship was that one had to explain nothing.*

– KATHERINE MANSFIELD

E

E

Name	Telephone
Address	

Name	Telephone
Address	

Name	Telephone
Address	

Name	Telephone
Address	

Name _____

Address _____

_____

_____

_____

Telephone _____

_____

_____

_____

Name _____

Address _____

_____

_____

_____

Telephone _____

_____

_____

_____

Name _____

Address _____

_____

_____

_____

Telephone _____

_____

_____

_____

Name _____

Address _____

_____

_____

_____

Telephone _____

_____

_____

_____

Shared joy is double joy, and shared sorrow is half-sorrow.

– SWEDISH PROVERB

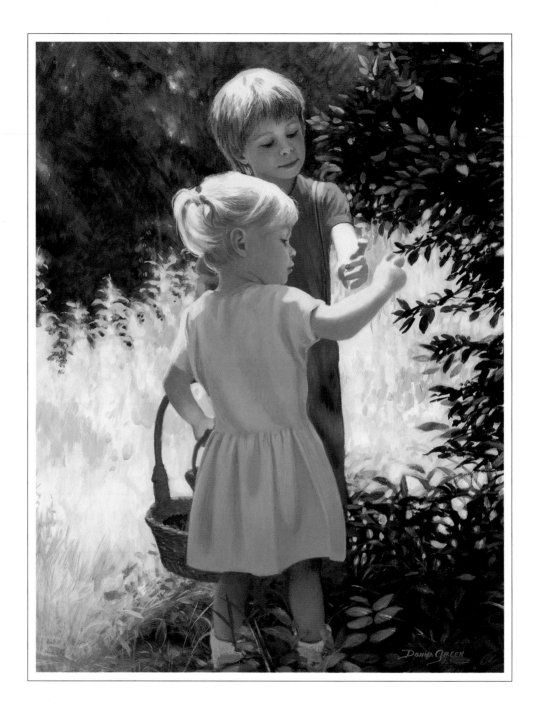

And the song from beginning to end, I found in the heart of a friend.

–HENRY WADSWORTH LONGFELLOW

Name

Telephone

Address

Name

Telephone

Address

Name

Telephone

Address

Name

Telephone

Address

Name

Telephone

Address

F

F

Name	Telephone
Address	

Name	Telephone
Address	

Name	Telephone
Address	

Name	Telephone
Address	

Name _____   Telephone _____

Address _____   _____

_____   _____

_____   _____

Name _____   Telephone _____

Address _____   _____

_____   _____

_____   _____

Name _____   Telephone _____

Address _____   _____

_____   _____

_____   _____

Name _____   Telephone _____

Address _____   _____

_____   _____

_____   _____

There was nothing remote or mysterious here – only something private.
The only secret was the ancient communication between two people.

– EUDORA WELTY

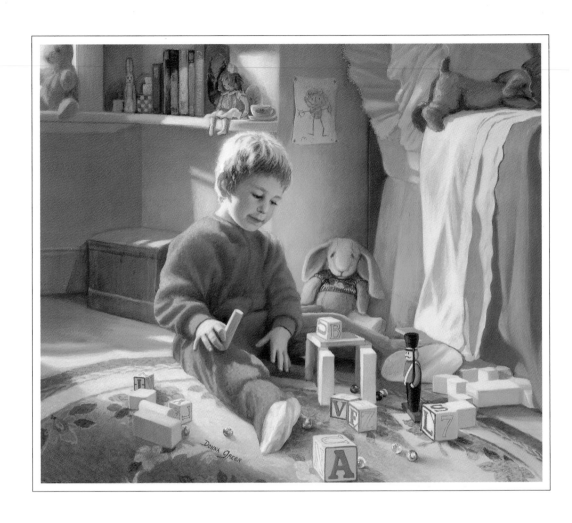

*I*s nothing in life ever straight and clear; the way children see it.

– ROSIE THOMAS

Name _____ *Telephone* _____

Address _____ _____

_____ _____

_____ _____

Name _____ *Telephone* _____

Address _____ _____

_____ _____

_____ _____

Name _____ *Telephone* _____

Address _____ _____

_____ _____

_____ _____

Name _____ *Telephone* _____

Address _____ _____

_____ _____

_____ _____

Name _____ *Telephone* _____

Address _____ _____

_____ _____

_____ _____

F

Name _____   Telephone _____

Address _____   _____

_____   _____

_____   _____

_____   _____

Name _____   Telephone _____

Address _____   _____

_____   _____

_____   _____

_____   _____

Name _____   Telephone _____

Address _____   _____

_____   _____

_____   _____

_____   _____

Name _____   Telephone _____

Address _____   _____

_____   _____

_____   _____

_____   _____

Name _____   Telephone _____

Address _____   _____

_____   _____

_____   _____

Name _____ *Telephone* _____

Address _____ _____

_____ _____

_____ _____

_____ _____

Name _____ *Telephone* _____

Address _____ _____

_____ _____

_____ _____

_____ _____

Name _____ *Telephone* _____

Address _____ _____

_____ _____

_____ _____

_____ _____

Name _____ *Telephone* _____

Address _____ _____

_____ _____

_____ _____

_____ _____

Name _____ *Telephone* _____

Address _____ _____

_____ _____

_____ _____

G

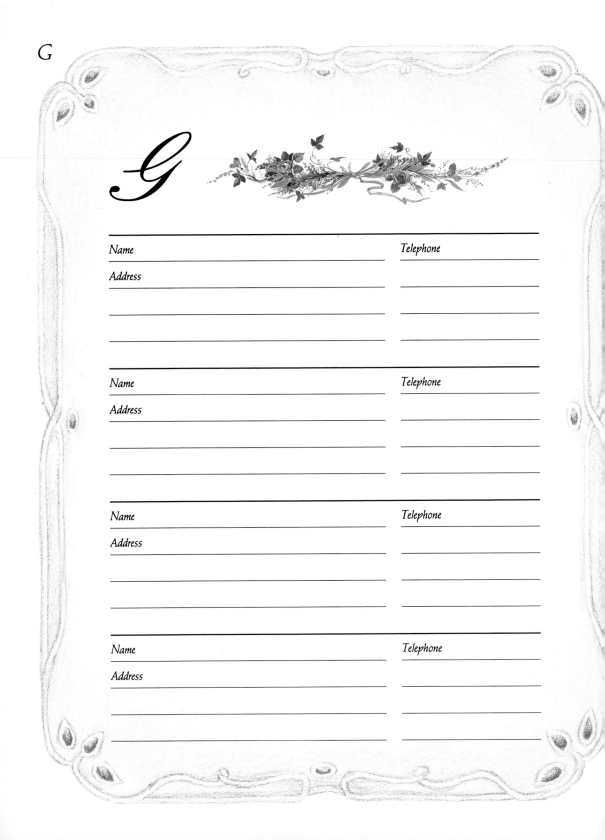

Name _____ Telephone _____

Address _____ _____

_____ _____

_____ _____

_____ _____

Name _____ Telephone _____

Address _____ _____

_____ _____

_____ _____

_____ _____

Name _____ Telephone _____

Address _____ _____

_____ _____

_____ _____

_____ _____

Name _____ Telephone _____

Address _____ _____

_____ _____

_____ _____

_____ _____

Name _____   Telephone _____

Address _____   _____

_____   _____

_____   _____

Name _____   Telephone _____

Address _____   _____

_____   _____

_____   _____

Name _____   Telephone _____

Address _____   _____

_____   _____

_____   _____

Name _____   Telephone _____

Address _____   _____

_____   _____

_____   _____

My friends are my estate. Forgive me then the avarice to hoard them. They tell me those who were poor early have different views of gold. I don't know how that is. God is not so wary as we, else He would give us no friends lest we forget him. — EMILY DICKINSON

If a child lives with criticism,
He learns to condemn.
If a child lives with hostility,
He learns to fight.
If a child lives with ridicule,
He learns to be shy.
If a child lives with shame,
He learns to feel guilty.
If a child lives with tolerance,
He learns to be patient.
If a child lives with encouragement,
He learns confidence.
If a child lives with fairness,
He learns justice.
If a child lives with security,
He learns to like himself.
If a child lives with acceptance and friendship,
He learns to find love in the world.

–DOROTHY L. NOLTE

Name   Telephone

Address

_____

_____

_____

Name   Telephone

Address

_____

_____

_____

Name   Telephone

Address

_____

_____

_____

Name   Telephone

Address

_____

_____

_____

Name   Telephone

Address

_____

_____

_____

Name _____   Telephone _____

Address _____   _____

_____   _____

_____   _____

_____   _____

Name _____   Telephone _____

Address _____   _____

_____   _____

_____   _____

_____   _____

Name _____   Telephone _____

Address _____   _____

_____   _____

_____   _____

_____   _____

Name _____   Telephone _____

Address _____   _____

_____   _____

_____   _____

Name _____   Telephone _____

Address _____   _____

_____   _____

_____   _____

Name _____   Telephone _____

Address _____   _____

_____   _____

_____   _____

Name _____   Telephone _____

Address _____   _____

_____   _____

_____   _____

Name _____   Telephone _____

Address _____   _____

_____   _____

_____   _____

*What the heart gives away is never gone . . . It is
kept in the hearts of others.*

–ROBIN ST. JOHN

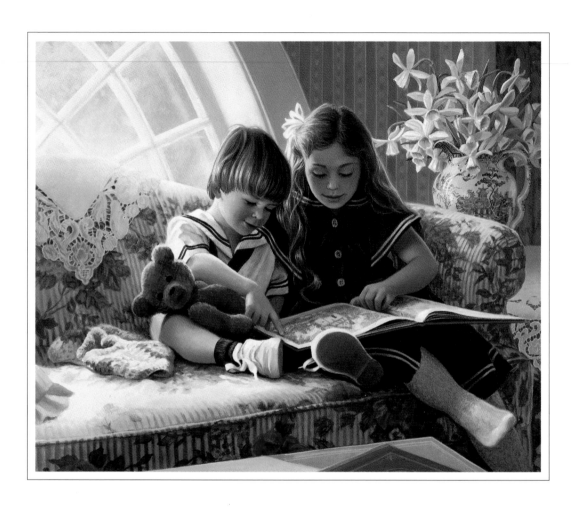

There is no frigate like a book to take us lands away
Nor any courses like a page of prancing poetry
This traverse may the poorest take without oppress of toil
How frugal is the chariot that bears the human soul!

– EMILY DICKINSON

Name _____ *Telephone* _____

Address _____ _____

_____ _____

_____ _____

Name _____ *Telephone* _____

Address _____ _____

_____ _____

_____ _____

Name _____ *Telephone* _____

Address _____ _____

_____ _____

_____ _____

Name _____ *Telephone* _____

Address _____ _____

_____ _____

_____ _____

Name _____ *Telephone* _____

Address _____ _____

_____ _____

_____ _____

I J

Name	Telephone
Address	

Name	Telephone
Address	

Name	Telephone
Address	

Name	Telephone
Address	

Name _____ Telephone _____

Address _____

_____ _____

_____ _____

Name _____ Telephone _____

Address _____

_____ _____

_____ _____

Name _____ Telephone _____

Address _____

_____ _____

_____ _____

Name _____ Telephone _____

Address _____

_____ _____

_____ _____

The healthy and strong individual is the one who asks for help when
he needs it, whether he's got an abscess on his knee or in his soul.

– RONA BARRET

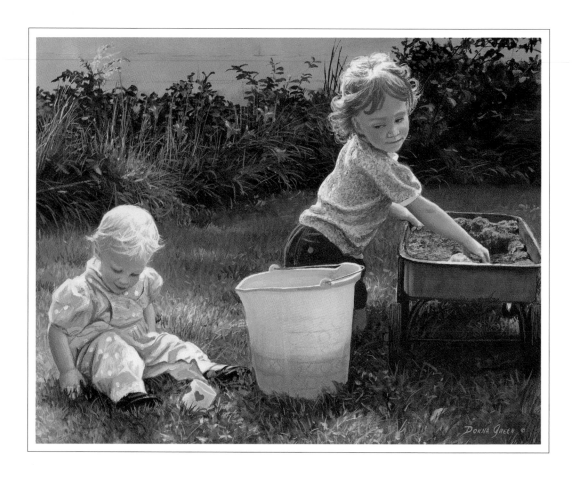

*S*ilences make the real conversations between friends. Not the
saying but the never needing to say is what counts.

– MARGARET LEE RUNBECK

Name

Telephone

Address

Name

Telephone

Address

Name

Telephone

Address

Name

Telephone

Address

Name

Telephone

Address

K

Name _____

Telephone _____

Address _____

_____

_____

_____

_____

_____

Name _____

Telephone _____

Address _____

_____

_____

_____

_____

_____

Name _____

Telephone _____

Address _____

_____

_____

_____

_____

_____

Name _____

Telephone _____

Address _____

_____

_____

_____

_____

_____

Name _____   Telephone _____

Address _____   _____

_____   _____

_____   _____

Name _____   Telephone _____

Address _____   _____

_____   _____

_____   _____

Name _____   Telephone _____

Address _____   _____

_____   _____

_____   _____

Name _____   Telephone _____

Address _____   _____

_____   _____

_____   _____

W*here you used to be, there is a hole in the world, which I find myself
constantly walking around in the daytime, and falling into at night.
I miss you like hell.* —EDNA ST. VINCENT MILLAY

K

Name _____ *Telephone* _____

Address _____ _____

_____ _____

_____ _____

Name _____ *Telephone* _____

Address _____ _____

_____ _____

_____ _____

Name _____ *Telephone* _____

Address _____ _____

_____ _____

_____ _____

Name _____ *Telephone* _____

Address _____ _____

_____ _____

_____ _____

Name _____ *Telephone* _____

Address _____ _____

_____ _____

_____ _____

*W*hat are little girls made of, made of?
What are little girls made of?
Sugar and spice, and all things nice,
That's what little girls are made of, made of.

– ANON

L

Name	*Telephone*
Address	

Name	*Telephone*
Address	

Name	*Telephone*
Address	

Name	*Telephone*
Address	

Name _____ Telephone _____

Address _____ _____

_____ _____

_____ _____

Name _____ Telephone _____

Address _____ _____

_____ _____

_____ _____

Name _____ Telephone _____

Address _____ _____

_____ _____

_____ _____

Name _____ Telephone _____

Address _____ _____

_____ _____

_____ _____

Constant use had not worn ragged the fabric of their friendship.
– DOROTHY PARKER

L

Name _____   *Telephone* _____

Address _____   _____

_____   _____

_____   _____

Name _____   *Telephone* _____

Address _____   _____

_____   _____

_____   _____

Name _____   *Telephone* _____

Address _____   _____

_____   _____

_____   _____

Name _____   *Telephone* _____

Address _____   _____

_____   _____

_____   _____

Name _____   *Telephone* _____

Address _____   _____

_____   _____

What are little boys made of, made of?
What are little boys made of?
Snips and snails, and puppy-dog's tails;
That's what little boys are made of, made of.

– ANON

L

Name _____ *Telephone* _____

Address _____ _____

_____ _____

_____ _____

_____ _____

Name _____ *Telephone* _____

Address _____ _____

_____ _____

_____ _____

_____ _____

Name _____ *Telephone* _____

Address _____ _____

_____ _____

_____ _____

_____ _____

Name _____ *Telephone* _____

Address _____ _____

_____ _____

_____ _____

_____ _____

Name _____   Telephone _____

Address _____   _____

_____   _____

_____   _____

_____   _____

Name _____   Telephone _____

Address _____   _____

_____   _____

_____   _____

Name _____   Telephone _____

Address _____   _____

_____   _____

_____   _____

Name _____   Telephone _____

Address _____   _____

_____   _____

_____   _____

One's life has value so long as one attributes value to the life of others, by means of love, friendship, indignation and compassion.

– SIMONE DE BEAUVOIR

M

Name _____   Telephone _____

Address _____   _____

_____   _____

_____   _____

Name _____   Telephone _____

Address _____   _____

_____   _____

_____   _____

Name _____   Telephone _____

Address _____   _____

_____   _____

_____   _____

Name _____   Telephone _____

Address _____   _____

_____   _____

_____   _____

Name _____ Telephone _____

Address _____ _____

_____ _____

_____ _____

Name _____ Telephone _____

Address _____ _____

_____ _____

_____ _____

Name _____ Telephone _____

Address _____ _____

_____ _____

_____ _____

Name _____ Telephone _____

Address _____ _____

_____ _____

_____ _____

Yes'm, old friends is always best, 'less you can catch a new one
that's fit to make an old one out of.

– SARAH ORNE JEWETT

M

Name	Telephone
Address	

Name	Telephone
Address	

Name	Telephone
Address	

Name	Telephone
Address	

Some of the finest friendships are between persons of different dispositions. The mind is often attracted by perfections it lacks itself.

– EUSTACE BUDGELL

Name

Telephone

Address

Name

Telephone

Address

Name

Telephone

Address

Name

Telephone

Address

Name

Telephone

Address

M

Name _____   *Telephone* _____

Address _____   _____

_____   _____

_____   _____

_____   _____

Name _____   *Telephone* _____

Address _____   _____

_____   _____

_____   _____

_____   _____

Name _____   *Telephone* _____

Address _____   _____

_____   _____

_____   _____

_____   _____

Name _____   *Telephone* _____

Address _____   _____

_____   _____

_____   _____

_____   _____

Name _____   *Telephone* _____

Address _____   _____

_____   _____

_____   _____

_____   _____

*E*ach friend represents a world in us, a world possibly not born
until they arrive, and it is only by this meeting that a new world
is born. — ANAÏS NIN

M

Name _____ *Telephone* _____

Address _____ _____

_____ _____

_____ _____

Name _____ *Telephone* _____

Address _____ _____

_____ _____

_____ _____

Name _____ *Telephone* _____

Address _____ _____

_____ _____

_____ _____

Name _____ *Telephone* _____

Address _____ _____

_____ _____

_____ _____

Name _____ *Telephone* _____

Address _____ _____

_____ _____

_____ _____

Name _____   Telephone _____

Address _____   _____

_____   _____

_____   _____

Name _____   Telephone _____

Address _____   _____

_____   _____

_____   _____

Name _____   Telephone _____

Address _____   _____

_____   _____

_____   _____

Name _____   Telephone _____

Address _____   _____

_____   _____

_____   _____

H*old a true friend with both your hands.*
– NIGERIAN PROVERB

N

N

Name	*Telephone*
Address	

Name	*Telephone*
Address	

Name	*Telephone*
Address	

Name	*Telephone*
Address	

Name _____   *Telephone* _____

Address _____   _____

_____   _____

_____   _____

Name _____   *Telephone* _____

Address _____   _____

_____   _____

_____   _____

Name _____   *Telephone* _____

Address _____   _____

_____   _____

_____   _____

Name _____   *Telephone* _____

Address _____   _____

_____   _____

_____   _____

T*he human heart, at whatever age, opens only to the heart that opens in return.*

– MARIE EDGEWORTH

Name

Telephone

Address

Name

Telephone

Address

Name

Telephone

Address

Name

Telephone

Address

Name

Telephone

Address

My only sketch, profile, of Heaven is a large blue sky, and larger
than the biggest I have seen in June – and in it are my friends –
every one of them.   – EMILY DICKINSON

N

Name

Address

Telephone

Name

Address

Telephone

Name

Address

Telephone

Name

Address

Telephone

Name

Address

Telephone

Name _____   Telephone _____

Address _____   _____

_____   _____

_____   _____

Name _____   Telephone _____

Address _____   _____

_____   _____

_____   _____

Name _____   Telephone _____

Address _____   _____

_____   _____

_____   _____

T*wo may talk together under the same roof for many years, yet never really meet; and two others at first speech are old friends.*

– MARY CATHERWOOD

O

O

Name _____   *Telephone* _____

Address _____   _____

_____   _____

_____   _____

Name _____   *Telephone* _____

Address _____   _____

_____   _____

_____   _____

Name _____   *Telephone* _____

Address _____   _____

_____   _____

_____   _____

Name _____   *Telephone* _____

Address _____   _____

_____   _____

_____   _____

Name _____

Address _____

_____

_____

Telephone _____

_____

_____

_____

Name _____

Address _____

_____

_____

Telephone _____

_____

_____

_____

Name _____

Address _____

_____

_____

Telephone _____

_____

_____

_____

Name _____

Address _____

_____

_____

Telephone _____

_____

_____

_____

A gentle word, like summer rain,
May soothe some heart and banish pain.
What joy or sadness often springs
From just the simple little things!

– WILLA HOEY

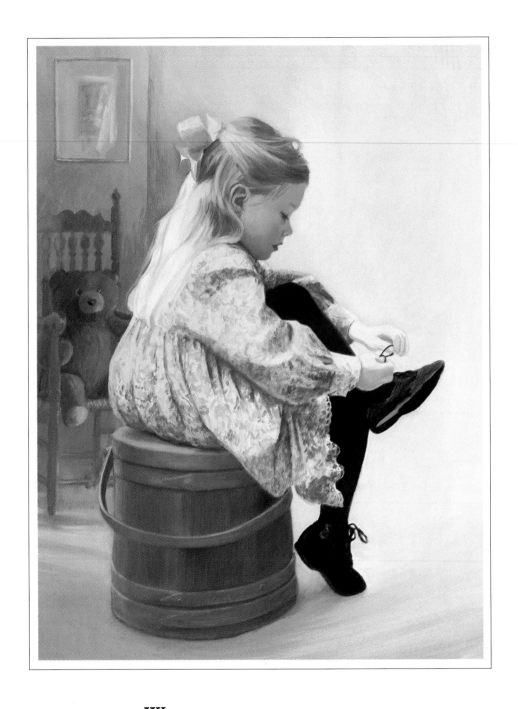

. . . *W*hat *do girls do who haven't any mothers to help them through their troubles?*

—LOUISA MAY ALCOTT

Name _____ Telephone _____

Address _____ _____

_____ _____

_____ _____

_____ _____

Name _____ Telephone _____

Address _____ _____

_____ _____

_____ _____

_____ _____

Name _____ Telephone _____

Address _____ _____

_____ _____

_____ _____

_____ _____

Name _____ Telephone _____

Address _____ _____

_____ _____

_____ _____

_____ _____

Name _____ Telephone _____

Address _____ _____

_____ _____

_____ _____

_____ _____

P

P

Name _____   *Telephone* _____

Address _____   _____

_____   _____

_____   _____

Name _____   *Telephone* _____

Address _____   _____

_____   _____

_____   _____

Name _____   *Telephone* _____

Address _____   _____

_____   _____

_____   _____

Name _____   *Telephone* _____

Address _____   _____

_____   _____

_____   _____

Name _____ Telephone _____

Address _____ _____

_____ _____

_____ _____

Name _____ Telephone _____

Address _____ _____

_____ _____

_____ _____

Name _____ Telephone _____

Address _____ _____

_____ _____

_____ _____

Name _____ Telephone _____

Address _____ _____

_____ _____

_____ _____

_____ _____

We cannot really love anybody with whom we never laugh.

– A. REPPLIER

P

Name _____   Telephone _____

Address _____

_____   _____

_____   _____

_____   _____

Name _____   Telephone _____

Address _____

_____   _____

_____   _____

_____   _____

Name _____   Telephone _____

Address _____

_____   _____

_____   _____

_____   _____

Name _____   Telephone _____

Address _____

_____   _____

_____   _____

Name _____   Telephone _____

Address _____

_____   _____

_____   _____

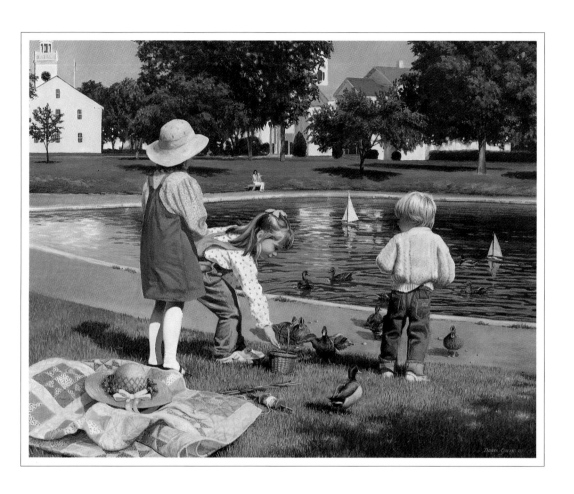

. . . *What do we live for if not to make the world less difficult for each other.*

–GEORGE ELIOT

P

Name _____ Telephone _____

Address _____ _____

_____ _____

_____

Name _____ Telephone _____

Address _____ _____

_____ _____

_____ _____

Name _____ Telephone _____

Address _____ _____

_____ _____

_____ _____

Name _____ Telephone _____

Address _____ _____

_____ _____

_____ _____

The truth is friendship is every bit as sacred and eternal as marriage.
– KATHERINE MANSFIELD

Name

Telephone

Address

Name

Telephone

Address

Name

Telephone

Address

Name

Telephone

Address

𝒬 𝓡

Name	*Telephone*
Address	

Name	*Telephone*
Address	

Name	*Telephone*
Address	

Name	*Telephone*
Address	

Name _____ Telephone _____

Address _____ _____

_____ _____

_____ _____

Name _____ Telephone _____

Address _____ _____

_____ _____

_____ _____

Name _____ Telephone _____

Address _____ _____

_____ _____

_____ _____

Name _____ Telephone _____

Address _____ _____

_____ _____

_____ _____

Treat your friends as you do your paintings,
and place them in the best light.

–JENNIE JEROME CHURCHILL

Q*R*

Name _____   *Telephone* _____

Address _____   _____

_____   _____

_____   _____

_____   _____

Name _____   *Telephone* _____

Address _____   _____

_____   _____

_____   _____

_____   _____

Name _____   *Telephone* _____

Address _____   _____

_____   _____

_____   _____

_____   _____

Name _____   *Telephone* _____

Address _____   _____

_____   _____

_____   _____

_____   _____

Name _____   *Telephone* _____

Address _____   _____

_____   _____

_____   _____

_____   _____

*T*he little things
That make life sweet
Are worth their weight in gold;
They can't be bought
At any price
And neither are they sold.
– ESTELLE WAITE HOOVER

Name _____ Telephone _____

Address _____ _____

_____ _____

_____ _____

Name _____ Telephone _____

Address _____ _____

_____ _____

_____ _____

_____ _____

Name _____ Telephone _____

Address _____ _____

_____ _____

_____ _____

_____ _____

Name _____ Telephone _____

Address _____ _____

_____ _____

_____ _____

_____ _____

Name _____ Telephone _____

Address _____ _____

_____ _____

_____ _____

Name

Telephone

Address

_____

_____

_____

Name

Telephone

Address

_____

_____

_____

Name

Telephone

Address

_____

_____

_____

Name

Telephone

Address

_____

_____

_____

If there is anything better than to be loved it is loving.

– ANON

S

Name   *Telephone*

Address

Name   *Telephone*

Address

Name   *Telephone*

Address

Name   *Telephone*

Address

Name _____ Telephone _____

Address _____ _____

_____ _____

_____ _____

Name _____ Telephone _____

Address _____ _____

_____ _____

_____ _____

Name _____ Telephone _____

Address _____ _____

_____ _____

_____ _____

Name _____ Telephone _____

Address _____ _____

_____ _____

_____ _____

That is the best - to laugh with someone because
you both think the same things are funny.
– GLORIA VANDERBILT

S

Name _____   Telephone _____

Address _____

_____

_____

_____

Name _____   Telephone _____

Address _____

_____

_____

_____

Name _____   Telephone _____

Address _____

_____

_____

_____

Name _____   Telephone _____

Address _____

_____

_____

_____

Name _____   Telephone _____

Address _____

_____

_____

Name _____   Telephone _____

Address _____   _____

_____   _____

_____   _____

Name _____   Telephone _____

Address _____   _____

_____   _____

_____   _____

Name _____   Telephone _____

Address _____   _____

_____   _____

_____   _____

Name _____   Telephone _____

Address _____   _____

_____   _____

_____   _____

Happiness is a sunbeam which may pass through a thousand bosoms without losing a particle of its original ray; nay, when it strikes on a kindred heart, like the converged light on a mirror, it reflects itself with redoubled brightness. It is not perfected till it is shared.

– JANE PORTER

Name

Telephone

Address

Name

Telephone

Address

Name

Telephone

Address

Name

Telephone

Address

Name

Telephone

Address

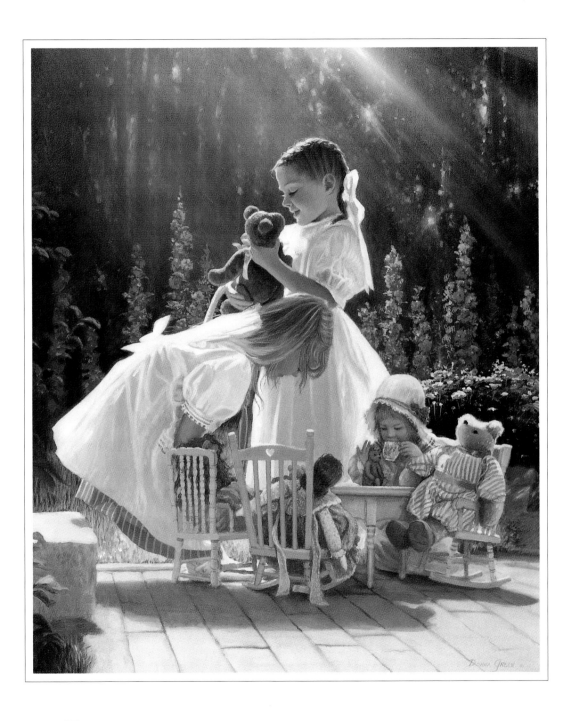

*T*he events of childhood do not pass but repeat themselves like seasons of the year.

– ELEANOR FARJEON

S

Name _____ *Telephone* _____

Address _____ _____

_____ _____

_____ _____

Name _____ *Telephone* _____

Address _____ _____

_____ _____

_____ _____

Name _____ *Telephone* _____

Address _____ _____

_____ _____

_____ _____

Name _____ *Telephone* _____

Address _____ _____

_____ _____

_____ _____

Name _____ *Telephone* _____

Address _____ _____

_____ _____

_____ _____

Name _____   Telephone _____

Address _____   _____

_____   _____

_____   _____

_____   _____

Name _____   Telephone _____

Address _____   _____

_____   _____

_____   _____

_____   _____

Name _____   Telephone _____

Address _____   _____

_____   _____

_____   _____

_____   _____

Name _____   Telephone _____

Address _____   _____

_____   _____

_____   _____

_____   _____

A *friend is one who knows all about you and likes you anyway.*
– CHRISTI MARY WARNER

T

T

Name _____ Telephone _____

Address _____ _____

_____ _____

_____ _____

Name _____ Telephone _____

Address _____ _____

_____ _____

_____ _____

Name _____ Telephone _____

Address _____ _____

_____ _____

_____ _____

Name _____ Telephone _____

Address _____ _____

_____ _____

_____ _____

Name _____   Telephone _____

Address _____   _____

_____   _____

_____   _____

Name _____   Telephone _____

Address _____   _____

_____   _____

_____   _____

Name _____   Telephone _____

Address _____   _____

_____   _____

_____   _____

Name _____   Telephone _____

Address _____   _____

_____   _____

_____   _____

Do not save your loving speeches
For your friends till they are dead;
Do not write them on their tombstones,
Speak them rather now instead.

– ANNA CUMMINS

T

Name _____   Telephone _____

Address _____   _____

_____   _____

_____   _____

Name _____   Telephone _____

Address _____   _____

_____   _____

_____   _____

Name _____   Telephone _____

Address _____   _____

_____   _____

_____   _____

Name _____   Telephone _____

Address _____   _____

_____   _____

_____   _____

In making dinner for a friend, don't forget the love.
–JEANNE MOREAU

Name

Address

Telephone

Name

Address

Telephone

Name

Address

Telephone

Name

Address

Telephone

Name

Address

Telephone

T

Name _____ Telephone _____

Address _____ _____

_____ _____

_____ _____

Name _____ Telephone _____

Address _____ _____

_____ _____

_____ _____

Name _____ Telephone _____

Address _____ _____

_____ _____

_____ _____

Name _____ Telephone _____

Address _____ _____

_____ _____

_____ _____

Name _____ Telephone _____

Address _____ _____

_____ _____

_____ _____

. . . *The companions of our childhood possess a certain power over our minds which hardly any later friend can obtain.*

– MARY SHELLEY

T

Name _____ *Telephone* _____

Address _____ _____

_____ _____

_____ _____

Name _____ *Telephone* _____

Address _____ _____

_____ _____

_____ _____

Name _____ *Telephone* _____

Address _____ _____

_____ _____

_____ _____

Name _____ *Telephone* _____

Address _____ _____

_____ _____

_____ _____

Name _____ *Telephone* _____

Address _____ _____

_____ _____

_____ _____

Name _____   *Telephone* _____

Address _____   _____

_____   _____

_____   _____

_____   _____

Name _____   *Telephone* _____

Address _____   _____

_____   _____

_____   _____

_____   _____

Name _____   *Telephone* _____

Address _____   _____

_____   _____

_____   _____

_____   _____

If I knew you and you knew me,
If both of us could clearly see,
And with an inner sight divine,
The meaning of your heart and mine,
I'm sure that we would differ less,
And clasp our hands in friendliness;
Our thoughts would pleasantly agree
If I knew you and you knew me.

–NIXON WATERMAN

U V

Name   Telephone

Address

Name   Telephone

Address

Name   Telephone

Address

Name   Telephone

Address

Name _____   Telephone _____

Address _____   _____

_____   _____

_____   _____

Name _____   Telephone _____

Address _____   _____

_____   _____

_____   _____

Name _____   Telephone _____

Address _____   _____

_____   _____

_____   _____

Name _____   Telephone _____

Address _____   _____

_____   _____

_____   _____

Kind words can be short and easy to speak,
but their echoes are truly endless.

– MOTHER TERESA

Name _____ Telephone _____

Address _____ _____

_____ _____

_____ _____

_____ _____

Name _____ Telephone _____

Address _____ _____

_____ _____

_____ _____

_____ _____

Name _____ Telephone _____

Address _____ _____

_____ _____

_____ _____

_____ _____

Name _____ Telephone _____

Address _____ _____

_____ _____

_____ _____

_____ _____

Name _____ Telephone _____

Address _____ _____

_____ _____

_____ _____

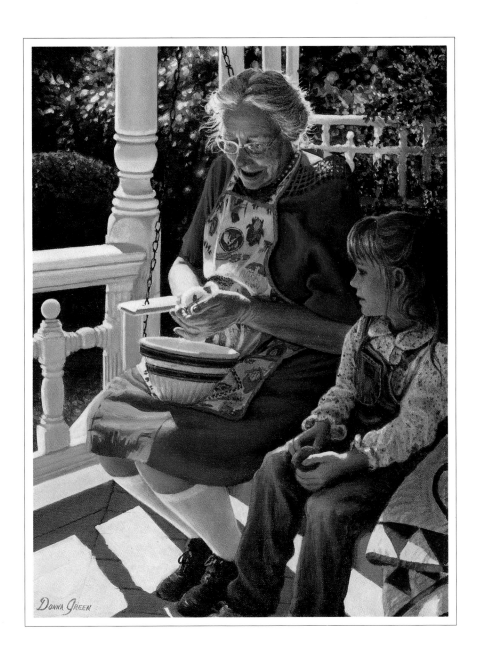

You may search my time-worn face,
*Y*ou'll find a merry eye that twinkles
I am NOT an old lady
Just a little girl with wrinkles!

— EDYTHE E. BREGNARD

W

Name _____   *Telephone* _____

Address _____   _____

_____   _____

_____   _____

Name _____   *Telephone* _____

Address _____   _____

_____   _____

_____   _____

Name _____   *Telephone* _____

Address _____   _____

_____   _____

_____   _____

Name _____   *Telephone* _____

Address _____   _____

_____   _____

_____   _____

Name _____   Telephone _____

Address _____   _____

_____   _____

_____   _____

Name _____   Telephone _____

Address _____   _____

_____   _____

_____   _____

Name _____   Telephone _____

Address _____   _____

_____   _____

_____   _____

Name _____   Telephone _____

Address _____   _____

_____   _____

_____   _____

Trouble is part of your life, and if you don't share it, you don't
give the person who loves you a chance to love you enough.

— DINAH SHORE

W

Name	*Telephone*
Address	

Name	*Telephone*
Address	

Name	*Telephone*
Address	

Name	*Telephone*
Address	

Name	*Telephone*
Address	

*T*here was a definite process by which one made people into friends, and it involved talking to them and listening to them for hours at a time.
— REBECCA WEST

W

Name _____   Telephone _____

Address _____   _____

_____   _____

_____   _____

Name _____   Telephone _____

Address _____   _____

_____   _____

_____   _____

Name _____   Telephone _____

Address _____   _____

_____   _____

_____   _____

Name _____   Telephone _____

Address _____   _____

_____   _____

_____   _____

Treasure each other in the recognition that we do
not know how long we shall have each other.

–JOSHUA LOTH LIEBMAN

W

Name _____   Telephone _____

Address _____   _____

_____   _____

_____   _____

Name _____   Telephone _____

Address _____   _____

_____   _____

_____   _____

Name _____   Telephone _____

Address _____   _____

_____   _____

_____   _____

Name _____   Telephone _____

Address _____   _____

_____   _____

_____   _____

Name _____   Telephone _____

Address _____   _____

_____   _____

_____   _____

X *Y* *Z*

Name _____   Telephone _____

Address _____   _____

_____   _____

_____   _____

_____   _____

Name _____   Telephone _____

Address _____   _____

_____   _____

_____   _____

_____   _____

Name _____   Telephone _____

Address _____   _____

_____   _____

_____   _____

_____   _____

Name _____   Telephone _____

Address _____   _____

_____   _____

_____   _____

Name

Telephone

Address

Name

Telephone

Address

Name

Telephone

Address

Name

Telephone

Address

The best and most beautiful things in the world cannot be seen or even touched. They must be felt with the heart.

– HELEN KELLER

XY^Z

Name

Telephone

Address

Name

Telephone

Address

Name

Telephone

Address

Name _____   Telephone _____

Address _____

_____

_____

_____

Name _____   Telephone _____

Address _____

_____

_____

_____

Name _____   Telephone _____

Address _____

_____

_____

_____

Name _____   Telephone _____

Address _____

_____

_____

_____

O*ne of the signs of passing youth is the birth of a sense of fellowship with other human beings as we take our place among them.*

– VIRGINIA WOOLF

XY^Z

Name _____ Telephone _____

Address _____ _____

_____ _____

_____ _____

Name _____ Telephone _____

Address _____ _____

_____ _____

_____ _____

Name _____ Telephone _____

Address _____ _____

_____ _____

_____ _____

Name _____ Telephone _____

Address _____ _____

_____ _____

_____ _____

Name _____ Telephone _____

Address _____ _____

_____ _____

_____ _____

Name

Telephone

Address

Name

Telephone

Address

Name

Telephone

Address

Name

Telephone

Address

But every road is rough to me that has no friend to cheer it.
– ELIZABETH SHANE

Notes

If I don't have friends, then I ain't got nothin'.

– BILLIE HOLIDAY

Notes

Notes

_____

_____

_____

_____

_____

_____

_____

_____

_____

_____

_____

_____

_____

_____

_____

There isn't much that I can do,
But I can sit an hour with you,
And I can share a joke with you,
And sometime share reverses, too . . .
As on our way we go.

— MAUDE PRESTON

Notes

_____

_____

_____

_____

_____

_____

_____

_____

_____

_____

_____

_____

The only thing to do is to hug one's friends tight and do one's job.

– EDITH WHARTON

Notes

Notes